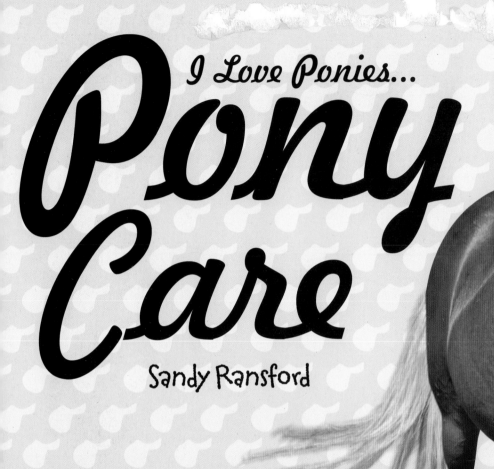

*I Love Ponies...*

# Pony Care

### Sandy Ransford

QED

Editor: Amanda Askew
Designer: Izzy Langridge

First published in the UK in 2011 by
QED Publishing
A Quarto Group company
226 City Road
London EC1V 2TT

www.qed-publishing.co.uk

A catalogue record for this book is available from the British Library.

ISBN 978 1 84835 661 0

Printed in China

**Remember!** Children must always wear appropriate clothing, including a riding hat, and follow safety guidelines when handling or riding horses and ponies.

**Picture credits**
(t=top, b=bottom, l=left, r=right, c=centre, fc=front cover)

All images are courtesy of Bob Langrish images unless stated below.

**Alamy** 10 Kenneth Ginn, 18br Norman Freelan
**Corbis** FC Stefanie Grewel
**DK Images** 11br Bob Langrish, 12 (water brush) Peter Chadwick,
(metal curry comb) Andy Crawford and Kit Houghton, 13l (1,2,3,4,5)
Kit Houghton, 13br Kit Houghton, 15 (1) Dorling Kindersley (2) Andy
Crawford and Kit Houghton, (3) Andy Crawford and Kit Houghton, (4)
Andy Crawford and Kit Houghton, (6) Andy Crawford and Kit Houghton,
19br David Handley
**Dreamstime** 12 (Rubber Curry Comb) Ad Van Brunschot, (body brush)
Stanko07
**Getty** 4 Melissa Farlow
**Shutterstock** 5b Pavel Kosek, 5t Lilac Mountain, 6t Maksym Protsenko,
6bl Chrislofoto, 7 (ragwort) Peter Wollinga, (yew) Joe Gough, (bracken)
Dariush M, (foxglove) J and S Photographhy, (rhododendron) Brykaylo
Yuriy, (deadly nightshade) Sue Robinson, (horsetail) LianeM, 7bc Judy
Kennamer, 8tr alessandro0770, 10tr marekuliasz, 12 (hoofpick) Cathleen
A Clapper, (sponge) Cretolamna, 15 (5) Mirecea BEZERGHEANU, 17cr Dennis Donohue, 21tr (injection)
Kondrashov Mlkhail Evgenevich, (sky) Serg64

Words in **bold** are explained in the glossary on page 22.

# Contents

# Basic pony needs

If you keep a pony, you need to give it food, water, shelter and company. Looking after it is hard work and takes up a lot of time.

Ponies are unhappy living on their own. If you have only one pony, it needs a companion, preferably another pony. However, they can also live with other animals such as sheep or goats.

## A place to live

You can keep a pony in a field, or partly in a stable and partly in a field. A pony would be unhappy inside all the time because it needs to be able to graze, roll and roam for at least part of each day. A stable provides shelter from the weather. A pony that lives in a field also needs shelter, such as trees or thick hedges.

Ponies will stand nose to tail in summer so they can swish the flies off each other's faces with their tails.

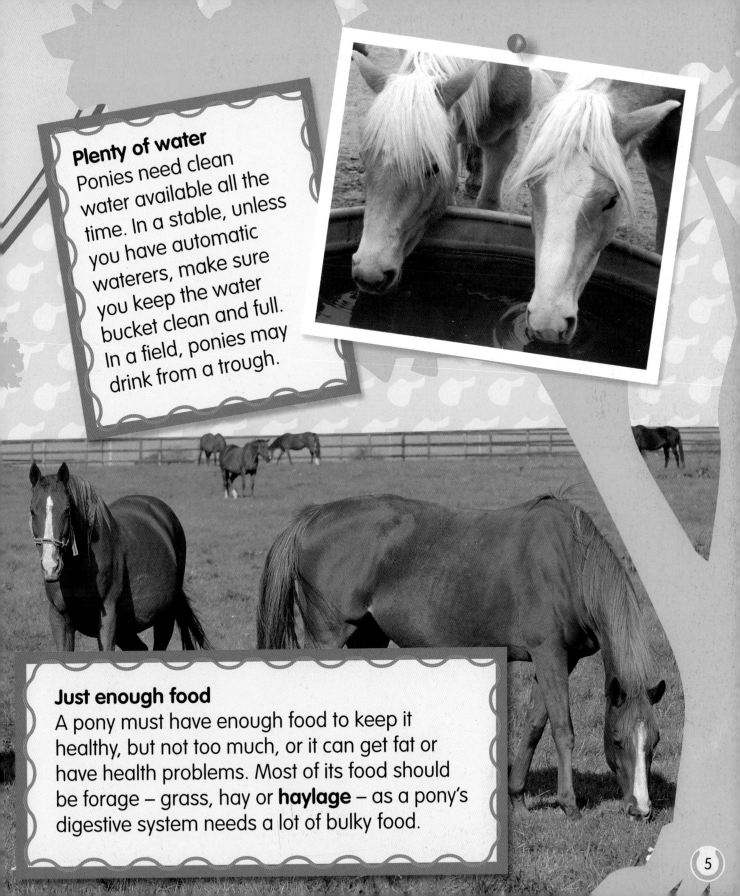

### Plenty of water

Ponies need clean water available all the time. In a stable, unless you have automatic waterers, make sure you keep the water bucket clean and full. In a field, ponies may drink from a trough.

### Just enough food

A pony must have enough food to keep it healthy, but not too much, or it can get fat or have health problems. Most of its food should be forage – grass, hay or **haylage** – as a pony's digestive system needs a lot of bulky food.

# Out in a field

A pony's field must have no poisonous plants, be properly fenced, provide shelter and have a clean water supply. The ground should not be boggy. The best kind of fencing is **post and rail**; the worst is barbed wire, especially if it is rusty and sagging.

A poor field        A good field

## Looking after the field

Ponies do not graze **paddocks** evenly. They eat some parts right down to the ground, and leave clumps of long grass in other places. To even out the grazing, leave the paddock empty from time to time, and then let sheep or cattle graze there. Two or three times a year, the field should be 'topped' – the tops taken off any weeds.

### Clued-up to care!

Keeping the field free of droppings helps prevent a pony from getting worms.

The field gate should hang properly and open and close easily. It should also be fastened securely so ponies cannot open it.

6

A trough fills automatically and saves a lot of work carrying water. It must be scrubbed out regularly to keep it clean.

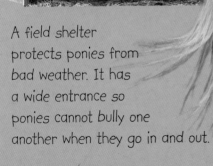

A field shelter protects ponies from bad weather. It has a wide entrance so ponies cannot bully one another when they go in and out.

## Poisonous plants

Ponies should not be put in a field where they can reach any of these plants.

ragwort

yew

bracken

foxglove

rhododendron

deadly nightshade

horsetail

# In a stable

An ideal stable is light and airy without being draughty. It should be big enough for the pony to move around freely.

Traditional stables have half-doors over which ponies can look out.

Sometimes stables are part of a barn, where several horses or ponies can be housed together.

### The building

A small pony can live in a stable measuring 3 by 3 metres; a larger pony needs more space. The floor needs a drainage system to take away liquid waste. Ponies need lots of fresh air, so the top half of the door should be left open. If the top parts of the windows open inwards, rain cannot blow in.

Switches and light bulbs should be where the pony cannot reach them.

You need a tying ring to hang a **haynet** and to tie the pony to when grooming.

### Bedding and mucking out
The stable needs a deep, dry bed for the pony to lie on. The bedding can be **straw**, shavings, baled newspaper or cardboard. You should muck out the stable every day – remove any droppings and wet bedding, and replace it with fresh bedding.

**Top tip!**
Manure and dirty bedding can be turned into compost for the garden.

# Feeding time

A pony's natural food is grass. It eats small amounts at a time, but spends many hours each day grazing, so it eats a lot over 24 hours. A pony should also be given extra food if it works hard.

### Hard feed
A hard-working pony needs **hard feed**, such as **coarse mix**, **pony nuts**, maize and sugar beet, two or three times a day. However, its main food should always be grass or hay (dried grass).

Coarse mix contains a mixture of grains and pony nuts.

Ponies grazing together in a field in winter can feed on piles of hay left on the ground. There should be more piles of hay than there are ponies, so the timid ones get a chance to eat.

### Soaking hay

Ponies can get coughs from the hay dust. To prevent this, soak the hay in water and then let it drain. You can use a dustbin for this. Be careful, a net full of wet hay is much heavier than a net full of dry hay.

### Watering

Ponies need clean, fresh water available all the time. If you do not have automatic waterers in the stable and the field, you must keep the buckets filled.

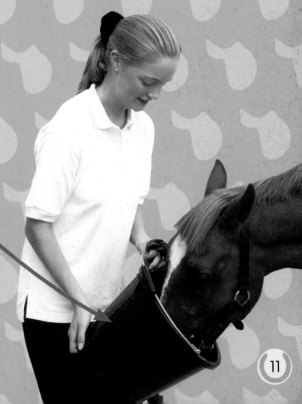

### Feeding routine

It's important to have a timetable for feeding a pony, and to stick to it. If the pony lives in a stable, it will expect breakfast at the same time every morning. It doesn't understand about weekends and holidays!

# Brush up!

You should keep your pony clean, but don't over-groom a pony that lives out. Grooming takes the grease out of its coat, which helps to keep it warm and dry.

**Grooming kit**

A water brush is used damp on the mane and tail to lay the hairs flat.

A hoofpick cleans out the feet.

A rubber curry comb removes dried mud and loose hairs.

Sponges are used for cleaning the eyes and nose, as well as the dock area.

A metal curry comb cleans the body brush.

A dandy brush removes dried mud, sweat and loose hairs.

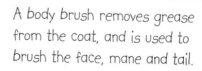

A body brush removes grease from the coat, and is used to brush the face, mane and tail.

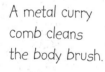

1

2

3

4

5

## Grooming a pony

**1.** When you groom a pony, start at its neck and work down its shoulders and front leg.

**2.** Do the other side, then slip off the **headcollar** while you carefully brush its face with the body brush.

**3.** Then brush its back, tummy and back legs.

**4.** Put the headcollar back on. Dampen the sponges, and clean round the eyes and nose with one, and the dock (the area under the tail) with another.

**5.** Finally, brush out the mane, forelock and tail with the body brush.

If you need to wash a pony's tail, do it in a bucket. Use a horse shampoo, and rinse the tail several times.

## Top tip!

To brush out the tail, hold it in one hand. Let go of a few hairs at a time and brush downwards with the body brush.

# Fancy footcare

It is very important for the pony's health that its feet are kept clean and are trimmed regularly by a **farrier**.

## Cleaning out the feet

To pick up a pony's foot, slide your hand down its leg, then tug at the fetlock hair and say, "Up." As the pony lifts its foot, slide your hand round to support it. Then, with the other hand, pick the dirt out of the foot with the hoofpick, using it from heel to toe. The feet should be picked out every day.

hoofpick

## Trimming the feet

A pony's hooves grow all the time, like your fingernails. They need trimming by a farrier every six to eight weeks, whether the pony wears shoes or not.

A front hoof wearing a shoe

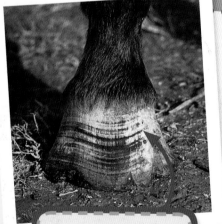

A neglected hoof in very poor condition

1. The farrier cuts the clenches (nail ends) and levers off the old shoe.

2. He trims the foot with hoofcutters.

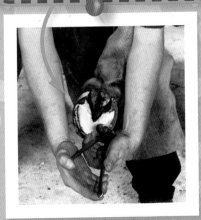

3. He rasps the foot to make it level.

## Shoeing a pony

If you ride a pony on roads and rough tracks, its feet wear down too quickly, so it needs shoes to protect them. A farrier removes the shoes to trim the feet, then either replaces them or puts on new ones.

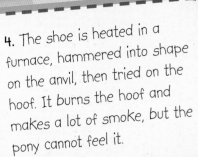

4. The shoe is heated in a furnace, hammered into shape on the anvil, then tried on the hoof. It burns the hoof and makes a lot of smoke, but the pony cannot feel it.

5. The shoe is cooled in a bucket of water before being nailed on.

6. The nails go in the underside of the foot and come out at the side.

# Weather watch

In winter and summer, you need to give your pony special care to cope with the weather.

## Winter feeding

Grass has little goodness in it during winter, so ponies need hay even if they live in a field. They may also need some hard feed.

In freezing weather, you have to break the ice on the water trough or bucket.

**Clipped** ponies, or ponies with fine coats, need to wear a special waterproof rug called a New Zealand rug, when out in the field.

Ponies can get sores on their heels and lower legs, called mud fever, in winter. Using special ointments can prevent this.

Straps round the back legs link together to help hold the rug in place.

When a pony works hard in winter, its coat is clipped off to stop it from sweating too much and losing condition. There are several different styles of clip. The trace clip (shown here) is the type used most often on ponies. A clipped pony needs to wear a rug in the stable as well as in the field.

## Summer shade

Ponies out in a field need shade from the hot summer sun. They also need protection from flies. It is best to stable them in the daytime in summer, and put them out at night. Those that are out in the daytime can wear a fly mask (shown here) or even a rug to keep off the flies.

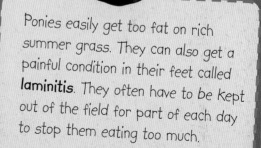

Ponies easily get too fat on rich summer grass. They can also get a painful condition in their feet called **laminitis**. They often have to be kept out of the field for part of each day to stop them eating too much.

# Care after riding

When you have finished your ride, you need to check that all is well with your pony before putting it back in the field or the stable. If you have worked your pony hard, it will be tired and hungry.

## Cooling down
If you bring a pony in hot and sweating after a ride and leave it standing around, it can get a chill. So always walk the last kilometre or so home to let it cool down.

## Removing the tack
Back at the stable, take off the pony's bridle and put on its headcollar. Then tie it up, and run the stirrups up the leathers, undo the girth and slide the saddle off the pony's back.

## Check the pony over
Brush off the saddle patch, and check the legs for any thorns or cuts. Check the feet for stones. If the legs are dry, brush off any mud.

Slide the saddle and the **numnah** back as you lift it off the pony's back to lay the hair flat.

## Sponging and brushing

In hot weather, you can sponge off the saddle patch with water and then dry it with a towel. In winter, especially if the pony is clipped, it must be kept warm. Cover its body with the rug while you brush it down, folding the rug back over the shoulders or the **quarters** to keep it out of the way.

## No gulping!

If the pony is hot and tired after working hard over a long day, just give it a small drink of tepid water at first. You can let it drink more later. Then give it a net of hay before its feed to stop it eating too quickly.

Giving water in a shallow container stops the pony from drinking too much at once.

Clued-up to care!
A pony likes to take its time drinking, lifting its head and then lowering it to drink again.

# Health care

You must look after a pony well to keep it healthy. It needs regular worming and vaccinations as well as exercise, fresh air and the right amount of food. Once you know what to look for, it is easy to tell the difference between a healthy and an ill pony.

### Fit and strong

A healthy pony has a shiny coat, bright eyes and is interested in everything going on around it. It will always be interested in food!

A well-cared-for pony in good health.

### Poorly and weak

A pony that is ill will have a dull coat. It may have dull eyes, a sad expression and may be thin, with its ribs sticking out.

An old, thin pony like this may need its teeth checked by a dentist.

## Colic

Colic is a pain in a pony's stomach. It can be serious, and you need to call the vet. Ponies with colic keep lying down to roll, then standing up again. They may turn round and snatch at their stomach with their teeth.

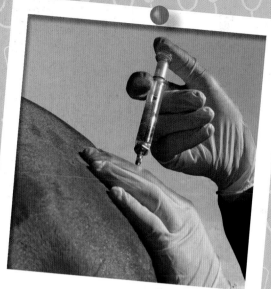

Ponies also need a vaccination each year to protect them from equine flu and tetanus.

A pony needs worming regularly. Medicine is mixed into its feed, or squirted onto its tongue. Worming kills parasites that live in the pony's intestines.

## Laminitis

Usually caused by over-eating, especially of spring and summer grass, laminitis gives a pony hot, painful feet, and makes it lame. A pony with laminitis often stands leaning back on its heels to try to take the weight off its toes.

# Glossary

**Clipped** When a pony's winter coat has been removed to stop it sweating when working hard.

**Coarse mix** A mixture of feed grains such as maize, barley, dried peas and beans.

**Farrier** Someone who trims horses' feet and shoes them.

**Hard feed** Concentrated cereals fed to a horse or pony in small quantities.

**Haylage** Grass which is cut and partly dried before being packed in bales.

**Haynet** Mesh bag in which hay is fed.

**Headcollar** Equipment that fits on a pony's head so you can lead it and tie it up.

**Laminitis** Inflammation of the insides of the pony's feet, making them hot and painful.

**Numnah** A pad used under the saddle to stop it from rubbing the pony's back.

**Paddock** Small field in which ponies are kept and sometimes ridden.

**Pony nuts** A kind of feed made from cereals compressed into small pellets.

**Post and rail** Fencing made from wooden rails (horizontals) fixed to wooden posts (uprights).

**Quarters** The part of a horse or pony behind the saddle.

**Straw** Hollow stalk of wheat, oats or barley, used as bedding.

# Index

# Notes for parents and teachers

Looking after a pony takes up a lot of time and can be very hard work. Ponies need attention at least twice a day, even if they live out in a field. Their diet needs careful regulation, and they like their meals at regular times. Every six to eight weeks their feet need trimming and if they are shod, they will need shoeing. Discuss with children the differences between caring for a pony, and caring for a cat or a dog.

Feeding a pony is very different from feeding most pets. Ponies have a small stomach and large intestines. They need small quantities of food almost constantly passing through their systems, so if they are not out eating grass, they need hay or haylage to chew on. Energy-giving grain feeds must only be provided in small quantities or they will upset the pony's digestion. Explain this to children, and contrast it with the way people eat.

Children may be worried about ponies feeling the more alarming parts of the shoeing process – the burning of the hoof and the hammering in of the nails. Explain that the hoof is just like your fingernails, and that the pony doesn't feel it, any more than you can feel cutting your nails.

Ask children to write a timetable for a day's pony care, starting with feeding in the early morning. They should then include turning the pony out in the field, mucking out the stable, grooming the pony, riding it, bringing it in at night, feeding it, and finally giving it a final haynet and check. Ask them if they'd like to carry out all these activities every day of the year, including in rain and winter snow.